KING
OF
IRON HEARTS

USA AND *WSJ* BESTSELLING AUTHOR

GIANA DARLING

KING OF IRON HEARTS
A collection of poems by Giana Darling
Writing as King Kyle Garro.

Copyright 2020 Giana Darling
Published by Giana Darling
Illustrations by Ali Silver
Edited by Jenny Sims
Cover design by Najla Qamber
Book design by Inkstain Design Studio

KING
OF
IRON HEARTS

CONTENTS

To all the women waiting for the man of their dreams.
And to the men patient enough to earn them.

The King of Iron Hearts
Is a fable now
A tale they tell children
About a man made of metal
Whose heart burned so boldly
It melted him from the inside out

WILD CARD

(KING)

Definition: a playing card that may have any
value or purpose determined by the player
holding the card in his or her hand.

WELCOME
TO THE
DARK SIDE

Welcome to the Dark Side
   Where the good go bad
   And the only lessons they teach
   Are those in corruption

THE
DEVIL

♥

The devil is a gentleman
    How else do you think
    He lured all those
    Sinning souls
    To hell?

SILVER TONGUED DEVILS

♥

People don't talk enough about devils
    With their silver tongues
    How the greatest sin they commit
    Is that thing they do
    With their precious metal mouths

OWN YOUR
DEMONS

I was born to the demons that hounded me.

They wanted my submission to their corruption like blood ink
on paper signed with my name.

I could have run,

But where is the power in that?

Instead, I became a demon myself in order to master them all.

Own your demons.

THE GOLDEN DEVIL

♥

The devil wasn't horns and talons
    Brimstone and ash.

He was golden and gorgeous
    Sinning and sex.

And I was his latest victim.

POWER
OF THE
NEGATIVE

♥

My mother thought I was a waste of space
    In her womb
    And the thought didn't improve when I was born.

My father thought I was a prince and raised me to be
    King.
    He had faith in everything I did.

My best friend didn't speak with words
    But everything he ever told me
    With his eyes and his actions
    Taught me I was worthy of love.

My sister told me once that our mother
    Educated her in self-hatred
    And steeped her deep in eternal doubt
    Because if a mother can't love her child
    Doesn't that make her right?

Why is it that the negative words of one
    Can so easily outweigh the good of every other?

THE LION

♥

A lion will never be a pet.
    You can put a collar on it,
    Lock it up at night,
    And call it pretty as much as you
    Want.
    But the real animal is you,
    For caging something that was meant to be
    Free.

Break up with your boyfriend.

RESPECT
YOUR ELDERS

♥

My father taught me with his fists
   My mother with her heavy sighs
   My uncle took me to church
   Where he taught me everything I should despise

My father hit me to keep me silent
   My mother didn't notice he was violent
   My uncle made me one of the choir boys
   Whom I discovered were all his toys

What happens when you are told to respect your elders, but they never show any respect for you?

BEHIND
THE GLASS

♥

Sometimes there is a two-way mirror
    Between you
    And the rest.
    Every day, you watch the others live their lives
    Talk, laugh, and touch
    A unit
    A family
    An entire world
    But
    Behind the glass
    You are alone
    Always
    Acutely unseen.

FAMILY
ISN'T BLOOD

♥

Family isn't in the blood
    It's the echo of each name
    That sounds with the beat of your heart.

BROTHER

Brother,
    You will never truly die
    Because
    Brother,
    I wear your friendship on my vest Like a badge.

Brother,
    When you went
    I thought about going with you
    But Brother,
    I knew you wouldn't want me.

Brother,
    I knew wherever you were
    Heaven, Hell, or Valhalla
    You were saving me a seat beside you
    When the time came for me to join you.

BROTHERHOOD

Brotherhood
    Is made by blood, sweat, and spit
    Forged in the fire of shared adversity
    Strong as titanium
    Common as iron
    Man-made

An awkward hug that lasts too long
    A secret handshake full of history
    A ride side by side connected by the wind
    Man-held

the respect of brothers
    the tightly knotted weave of friendship
    something more than family
    something beautiful that only exists between
    Man to man

THE BALANCE

♥

It's the balance she craves.

The soft core under immovable steel
    The rough against the slide of silky skin
    The coarse voice speaking in dulcet tones

A woman wants a man like a weapon
    That could never be turned against her
    One only she can wield
    When she needs that strength to be her sword
    And his love her shield

BEING BAD

♥

I just like being bad

The guy people don't get
    The one they want to fuck
    The one they don't want to fight
    And the one you just can't kill

I just like being bad
    A man with the road beneath his bike
    And the taste of whiskey on his breath
    The one who kisses like he brawls
    Who walks with a 'I gotta secret' kinda swagger

I just like being bad
>   But more than that, I like being bad for you
>   My good girl with a taste for something wild
>   You can suck the danger from my lips
>   While I keep you safe in my arms
>   Because no one fucks with you
>   Not even me

How the bad boy gets the girl.

COWBOY BLUES

I've been a cowboy my whole life
    Workin' to wrangle
    A soul so wild
    It bucks against the red ropes that bind it
    Knocks into the bone bars that cage it

I've been keepin' it steady for so many years
    Just waitin' for you to walk on by
    And bring it to heel with the swish of your hair
    And the sight of your smile.

LIKE CHERRIES

❤

Behind her ears
    The gentle slope of her neck
    The underside of her jaw
    I want to know how she tastes
    But I am already convinced
    She tastes like cherries

A DIFFERENT PRETTY

♥

There was nothing gentle in her beauty
   Nothing soft or romantic

She was an exclamation mark

The study of her exquisiteness punctuated by
   A punch to the solar plexus

A different kind of pretty.

ART OF D&S

♥

Sometimes a wild soul
Doesn't yearn for open fields

It wants strong hands and stern words
To break under hard rules

Until the restless chaos in their hearts is soothed
Their loud spirit is quiet
And for a moment, blissfully at peace.

The art of Domination and submission.

QUEEN
OF THE
JUNGLE

♥

Sometimes I catch my daughter watching the animal channel, her hands curled into claws and her lips pulled back to reveal tiny teeth. She growls sometimes, but nothing prepares me for the eventual ferocity of her roar.

When I ask her what she's doing, she breaks character to smile and say, "I'm learning how to be like mummy, fierce and loyal, strong and beautiful in a way that people respect "

"I want to be queen of the jungle."

A MAN

♥

A man should show strength
    Power in his veins like burning live wires
    Crackled intensity inside his gaze
    Spiralling up the rod of steel in his spine

But
    There are tears in my ducts
    Caught in the velvet pink like jewels
    They gleam
    Betraying me
    My spine wilts
    Metal melting in the firestorm
    Of my flaming heart
    That burns
    Like some eternal torch
    Stronger than my manliness
    More powerful than my might
    It wrecks me weak from the inside out

Machismo

REBEL WITH
A CAUSE

Dirt in my boots
    Ink on my hands and a bike
    Thrum
    Humming between my legs

Bad boy
    Sinner
    Future criminal

But I have love on the brain
    And stars in my eyes my father pulled
    From the sky just for me

I have words on my tongue
    That gather like pearls
    And when I speak
    It's in jeweled prose

Are my gems precious enough for you?
    Even with mud on my face and iron in my blood.

I may be a rebel, but I'm one with a cause.
    And that cause is you.

CHAOS

I have an insatiable appetite for destruction
    An incurable need for a simple view
    To fracture like a kaleidoscope
    Into so much colour
    So many shapes
    Until what once was
    Is now so much more

PRETTY BOY

♥

Pretty boy
> They all want you
> The girls with dips and curves
> For hand holds
> The thin young things with
> Eager lips

All the women see a man
> Tall, dark, and handsome
> With an edge
> Drawn in ink on his skin
> And they want you

Pretty boy
> You collect them all
> The redheads, the blondes
> And the mahogany haired
> Like notches on your belt

But the one girl who sees
    The chemistry of your plastic smile
    And the depth of your hollow gaze
    The one girl who sees more than just
    A pretty boy
    You keep her far away

MUTE

I may be mute
    Because I do not have the words
    To express the depthless font of feelings
    In my dark and twisted heart
    But do not assume
    That makes me blind as well

I WAS MUTE

❤

I was mute
  In class
  Silent
  At parties
  So quiet in my throat
  It spread like a virus into my lungs
  Over my skin and hair
  Until it was a physical thing
  Invisibility
  Yet
  You noticed me
  And your voice
  It outlined my edges
  Filled in my blanks with colours
  You
  You noticed me
  And in the beauty of that regard
  I found my voice

Because I needed one to describe
The wet blue velvet in your eyes
And the thin skin where your thigh meets
Your groin that is sweet and velvet as a bruised peach
I learned
To speak with words
That could only be heard
With my lips pressed to your flesh

I'M A STORM

♥

"I'm a storm," you said.
    "Gale force winds and pelting rains
    Sudden explosions of noise and wet
    So much thunder
    You roar
    You cannot contain me
    I cannot be yours."

But I am a storm chaser
    Hurricane watcher
    I don't need to catch you to claim you
    I only need to respect you to love you.

SATAN

Why is there no sympathy for the devil?

He who sits in irons bound to a dark throne
    In a kingdom filled with hate and loss
    Stinking of brimstone

He who has the company of demons and sinners
    Who rules over an endless growing domain
    That echoes with wraith's pitiful moans and wails

Why is there no sympathy for the immortal man?
    Who paid for the simple sin of pride
    With an eternity of ruling restless souls
    That will never love his own?

HOUSE
OF
CARDS

(KING)

Definition: a plan or purpose with an unstable
structure the could be destroyed easily.

NOT FORGOTTEN

There is so much poetry in devastation
    In the monumental destruction of things
    Of ancient pyramids falling broken in the sands
    Of grand empires fracturing into modern states
    Some things break beyond compare
    But there is worth to be found in the archeology
    Of those ruins

Everything lost is not forgotten.

WHY IS IT?

♥

Why is it
    That you hurt me so bad
    And the only person I want
    To comfort me
    Is you?

FRANKENSTEIN
THE
MONSTER

♥

Have you considered
    That it was Dr. Frankenstein who was
    The real monster?

We are the product of our circumstances.

MONSTER

Why is a monster a monster?

Because it doesn't know how to retract its claws.

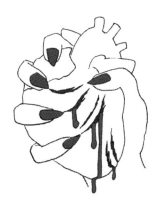

A SAD EDUCATION

I am old sorrow
    Ancient tears that have dried on the shore
    Between the creases of each rock like sad diamonds
    Barely winking in the cloud-filtered light.

I am withered dreams
    Empty husks dashed upon dry soil
    That has yet to be tilled
    A fallow moment in time
    Momentarily forgotten.

I am fossilized heartbreak
    Whorls of my fractured soul
    Trapped in hardened fragments of soil
    Compressed by time
    For other people to find and study
    That they might learn from my mistakes.

PHANTOM LIMB

♥

How can 'what-if'
     Feel like a war wound
     From a battle you forgot you fought
     A limb you never really lost
     That feels as though it's gone

SHE
WALKED BY

♥

She walked by me
    So many times
    Without seeing me
    But I saw her
    So many times
    Without even looking

She was etched onto my lids
    Scent punctured through my nostrils
    Voice looped through my head like a song
    I was branded by the sight of her
    While she…
    She didn't even know my name.

UNREQUITED

The greatest tragedy
    Of unrequited love
    Is knowing
    You have an expensive gift to give That will never be received
    No matter how charmingly you wrap it
    Or how often you lay it at their door
    It will remain forever unopened
    Unwanted
    And insecure.

We are sorry to inform you, your application has been denied.

HEAD
IN THE
CLOUDS

To all the girls with their heads in the clouds
    Don't forget to draw down the dream you wish there
    Like a balloon pulled from the sky
    And carry it with you while
    You walk down the street
    So you might notice me finally when I find you there

PENNY WISH

I felt like a penny
    Picked up, rubbed clean, and then used
    To make a wish for something more.

CHANGE
THE WAY

♥

Why did you have to change the way
   You loved me?

Because you wanted to be best?
   Closest?
   More secure?

Why did you have to change the way
   You spoke to me?
   Because I couldn't love you back the way
   You wanted?
   And it made you bitter
   Turned you toxic?

Why did you have to change the way
    You touched me?
    The hand once around my shoulder sliding
    Down the crease of my inner thigh
    Pulling me close when you should have pushed me away
    Because now your lust was in our way

Why did you have to change the way
    You loved me?
    Because now,
    It is impossible for me to love you back.

ONE
MOMENT
& THE
NEXT

It is its own kind of miracle

How someone can look at you

Like you have hung the silver moon

In the velvet sky of their most luxurious dreams

One moment

And

The next

They never want to see you

Again

ROMANCE
NOVELS

♥

Romance novels made me an insomniac
    I waited by the phone in the darkest hours
    Held my breath until the silence mocked me
    And the emptiness of the room without you
    Began to echo

OVERRIPE

♥

Overripe with love
    You fall from the limb
    Too ready
    Too willing to be had
    You break open on the ground
    Only food for the flies

RUST OVER TIME

You were moonlit sonatas
   And the stars in the sky
   We were young and hopeless with wishes tied to clouds
   Like children's balloons
   We didn't know they were so
   Fragile
   That close to the heavens
   We didn't know
   That even stardust could rust over time

ANYTHING FOR LOVE

♥

Anything for love
    They say
    Let that count for love of self too
    If your soul cries out for it
    It's not selfish
    It's sustenance

WORTHY

♥

Don't settle for friendship
    When you need love

Don't settle for sometimes
    When you deserve someone's always

You have the worth you give yourself

YOUR CURRENCY

♥

Your worth is not measured by the angle of your hips
    And the gap between your thighs
    In the weight of your breasts
    And the breadth of your smile.
    It's hidden shyly in the corners of your face
    For few to find.
    A flower safe guarded in the middle
    Of a book you have to study
    Before you find the prize.

The true currency of your glamour.

SOUL SO
PRETTY

Sometimes a person's got a soul so pretty
It makes them glow prettier than anything else.

Lust is no true substitute for pure care.

ENTIRE
GALAXY

I have an entire galaxy in my soul
   And you have only landed on the moon
   Do not think
   Because you can see my stars
   That you have earned the right to colonize them

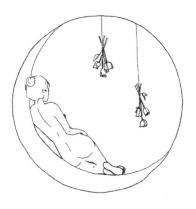

GUTTED

♥

You pushed and pulled
    Breaking apart an old house
    Thinking you wanted what was in it
    All the baggage you thought was treasure

Finally
    The boards cracked under your pressure And I broke open
    Just the way you wanted
    Exactly what you worked for
    All my secrets
    And my troubles
    My old house aches and pains
    At your feet for you to pilfer.

We didn't speak after that.

BLACK HOLE

There is a black hole at the center of every universe.
　It yawns
　Stretches
　And contracts
　But it is constant
　Ever hungry.

So,
　You feed it.
　Sweet bursts of sugar
　Deep draughts of the finest wine.
　You fill it with vicious violence and
　Blood red rage
　With sex and sinning
　Envy and greed.
　It eats
　And eats

Everything you give it
But sometimes
The right times
All it takes is a mirror to prop before it
And it doesn't seem so depthless after all.

What do you feed your demons?

LIES

Remember
    It is you who makes a lie come alive.

Someone need only sow the seed
    In the fertile field of your mind
    Where they might watch it take root
    In your insecurities
    Flourish under the drizzle of your fears
    And blossom in the sunny belief you hold
    For anyone who lets you love them.

This is how a lie takes hold.

FRIENDSHIP
LOVE LETTER

♥

There are not enough love letters about friendship
    How it feels to know you have a home
    Inside the heart of another being
    They are the kerchief for your tears
    The arms around your shaking shoulders
    The hands that help carry your burdens

There are not enough love letters about friendship
    Yet they suffer the same betrayals
    And nothing is as brutal as a knife in the back
    From a person you trusted with all your pain

THE WORST
MONSTERS

♥

I've found
  That the worst monsters
  Have the prettiest faces

The art of deception.

BITTER HATE

His laugh was bitter and sharp with hate
I swallowed it down like hemlock
And wondered how long it would take

ALL YOUR FLAWS

♥

I have an encyclopedic knowledge
    Of all your flaws
    I ripped out the pages
    Of things to love
    Verbs of worship and nouns that rhyme
    With your name
    I burned the edges of the Holy Bible
    Because you once told me
    God wasn't as important as our love
    And in the end,
    It was the biggest lie you ever told

HATE IS
PRETTY

♥

Love looks best on you
But honestly,
Hate is pretty too.

ANGER
LIKE A
GARDEN

♥

She tends to her anger like a garden

Waters the earth with her hot salt tears
    So that only red flowers can bloom
    Poppies to commemorate a violent death
    Of something she once held so dear

Digs up the weeds with her bare hands
    And bleeding, broken nails
    So that her skin is stained just as dark
    As the bruises she secrets away on her heart

She tends to her garden of ivy and wrath
    Like a groundskeeper
    For an estate of eternal hate

MIDAS
OF DEATH

♥

The Midas of death

I turn everything I touch to ash

All the beautiful things reduced to soot beneath my fingernails
    But
    Still I reach for that golden thing
    That indelible light of life

Even knowing
    The press of one finger
    Will blow it all to smoke.

THE BREAK UP

No one ever speaks
    About the heartbreak
    Of shattering another's dreams
    Of taking the love they have for you
    And stamping it
    Cannot be delivered.
    Return to sender.
    Just because I am the one who broke
    Your heart
    It does not mean
    I didn't rip off a little piece of my soul
    In the process

The break up.

AN ARSONIST

♥

Is there beauty in ashes?
   Because I am razed to the ground
   Burnt up by my own flames
   An arsonist
   With a self-fulfilling destiny

TOXIC

Who knew love could be so toxic?

That the flames they spoke of wouldn't set my heart on fire
or heat my groin like warm coals.

That instead it would eat me up to ash like lit paper
   Until I crumbled into dust.

SHE HURTS ME

♥

Yes, she hurts me

She knows I love her because I bleed for her whenever she needs proof
   She knows because I fight for her even against myself
   She knows because I fell in love with her at eight and never
   stopped

But the cruel agony of life
   Is that I will never know for sure
   How much she loves me back
   Because no one ever taught her how
   Or gave her the courage to try.

Sometimes love stories don't work out.

HEARTBREAK CRIME SCENE

♥

I stood in a pool of blood
    At the scene of my heartbreak
    And wondered if the blue and red lights
    Flashing across the carnage
    Could make sense of the sorrow
    That brutalized my chest
    As wide and gory as a shotgun wound.

Would they itemize the reasons?
    Surmise the motive
    And write a report
    So succinct
    I would read it and
    Not feel the horror of those events
    Again in my heart?

The police work of therapy.

LAW OF
OPPOSITES

♥

They say opposites attract
    But what if
    We really are polar opposites?
    If our currents run at perpendicular angles and our
    frequen-cies on different channels
    What if we want to love each other
    But the Law of Physics disproves it?

NEVER
CONNECT

♥

Our bodies were magnetic
    The energy between our skin
    Was so strong
    We couldn't bear to be apart

But our hearts were polarized
    Too contrary to coexist
    So even when our bodies collided
    Our souls could never connect

TOO LATE

She was whelved so deeply in the tissues and chambers of my heart
it took me years to find her
 And by then, it was too late.

SEASONS
OF THE
HEART

All her life
    You planted flowers under her skin
    A poppy on her throat
    Handfuls of peonies across her hips
    A tropical paradise warm and wet
    At her core
    You planted lust and desire in blooms
    And plumes of green leaves
    All over her body
    You planted a garden in her heart
    But didn't stop to watch it grow
    Or smell the flowers as you passed
    That blossomed just for you

Seasons of the heart.

TWO SOULS

To watch them was to know
    That two souls could be perfectly matched
    Harmoniously in tune
    Seamlessly entangled
    And somehow
    Never know it

YO-YO LOVE

♥

You dropped me
    But I wanted to snap back
    Like a yo-yo
    Into your hand
    Even if it meant
    You would drop me
    Again

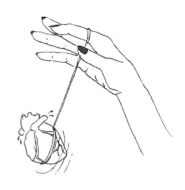

MY FAIRYTALE

I fought for my fairytale
And in the end
My prince was the villain
And I was a hero

LITTLE LADY

♥

Corners meet
    Dark nesting in their folds
    Harbouring the fragile glow of a woman
    And I ask you then,
    How do you see me?

As a creature of the moon
    Refracting a light not lost
    But glimmering
    A soft broken piece of ancient clay
    Submerged in burning fluid
    That eats with tearing teeth at flesh and thought
    Until
    I sit a creature of the moon disowned
    In human sin

Do you know me as a little lady?
    With milk froth of petticoats
    Stained by rusty human oil
    Doll hands clutching
    To the broken fingers of grace
    Stunted growth now curling over like spoiled time
    In shame
    Know me as the little lady fallen off
    A high sharp shoe

Would you want me as a naked woman lies?
    Curving broken back to arch
    Groaning desperate desire
    From a throat painted with crimson lines
    Of your love
    Tasting like honeyed cream
    Without the blemish of tattooed bluebells and overripe plums
    Want me as I lay a woman
    Exposed lines folds and hand holds
    Not as naked as you'd like

Could you love me as I am?
    Like a soft child's lullaby of
    Glimmering shimmering gold
    Like a masterful David to look at and lust
    But only wonder at in gentle curiosity

As not the naked woman lies
        As not the little lady knows
        As not the creature of the moon
        But more a person of her own

Then how do you see me?
        As I crouch in a corner of shadow's nest
        Licking and lapping at metallic red to
        Stop the human oil slick
        And soothe the sore lace torn flesh
        Back curved in not lust for you
        But pain
        How do you see me now, my love?

STREET
POETRY

Street poetry
> Written in graffiti and waste
> One man's garbage is another's taste

The art of being thrown away.

I COULDN'T
HAVE YOU

♥

I couldn't have you so
　　We stopped speaking.

I couldn't avoid you so
　　I moved to another country.

I couldn't forget you so
　　I married another woman
　　Dreamt of you each night
　　And woke up with her each morning.

I couldn't have you yet
　　Even across all that ocean
　　With all that time between us
　　And me
　　I was still doomed to love you.

A WISH

♥

A wish is a seed
    Something to plant and germinate
    Something to nurture and grow
    They teach you in grade school
    Water, sunshine, soil
    And *poof*
    A plant
    I thought hope was like that
    Love was like that
    And while I had the seed to sow
    You gave me nothing to feed it

I am a fallow field.

RAIN
JUST FALLS

I kept waiting for all the dirt and rain
    Of my life
    To blossom into flowers
    But I guess
    Sometimes
    Dirt is just grime
    And rain just falls

NATURAL REMEDY

♥

So many men try to drown their misery at the bottom
 Of a bottle.

Why don't they try to drown it in the rain?
 Or trap it in prose at the bottom of that bottle
 And drown it in the sea.

The natural remedy for all maladies.

UP
THE
ANTE
(KING)

Definition: increase the stakes, especially
in times of dispute or conflict

THE SERPENT

♥

I don't want to be the phoenix
    I want to be the serpent

The snake is not
    The sly evil thing in the grass
    Of Eden's garden

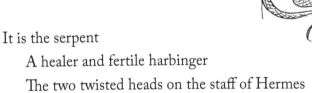

It is the serpent
    A healer and fertile harbinger
    The two twisted heads on the staff of Hermes

The serpent is the middle of black and white
    The dual expression of good and evil

The serpent does not die and is reborn anew
    The serpent evolves, changes, and grows
    Shedding the skin of the past but retaining the memory
    So that when it slithers forward it does it wise

SACRIFICIAL LAMB

♥

She was sharp as a heart attack
    A woman in need of sacrifice
    And reverence
    Who understood her worth
    And demanded payment
    For her venerable affections

I capitulated to the fury of her need
    Cut my heart out of my chest with her dagger
    Rusty with old blood
    The stain of other lovers
    Who had failed to fill her greed

I handed it to her
    Still beating
    Thumping against the silver platter
    Like a war drum
    She looked me in the eye as she took it
    In one pale hand
    Raised it to her lips and licked the aorta
    Until it throbbed
    "I will consume you whole."
    She promised.

The man is the sacrificial lamb in this one.

SLAYED
DEMONS

♥

I slayed my demons
    With my bare hands
    Stuffed the heads
    And mounted them on my wall
    So that anytime I was frightened
    Anytime I felt threatened
    I could look in the eyes of my villains
    And remember
    I had the power to end them

THE BEAST

What if the beast in the story
    Preferred his talons and fangs
    And the echo of his mighty roar

What if he enjoyed striking fear into hearts
    So they never again had a chance to hurt his own?

The beast stays a beast in this one.

CRUEL MAN
IN LOVE

♥

My love is a fist
 Clenched hard
 Inflexible
 Impossible to miss
 When it hits you in the face

My love is a dagger
 Cold edged steel
 Sharp
 I use it to carve scars
 In your skin that spell my name

I remain a cruel man
 Uncaring
 A villain at ease in his skin
 But my love for you is kind

If that isn't magic, what is?

DRAGONS

Not all princesses need Prince Charmings to save them
  Sometimes
  They have dragons who protected them
  All along

AN EDGE
TO FALL OFF

♥

I am at ease with hatred
    Comfortable with deviance
    And friendly with rebellion
    I wear my wrath like a leather coat
    And my venom is a cloud of second-hand smoke

You see me and want me
    Do you know why?
    Because I am the edge you need to fall off
    The adrenaline rush you want to try

TOO CLOSE
TO DEATH

♥

I am too close to Death.

He hounds me like a loyal shadow
 Whispers dark delights in my ear.

I am his friend.
 Disciple.

I learn from him the way to take men apart
 Like dissembling a tool.

They learn to fear me too.
 A walking nightmare in motorcycle boots.

But what about you, sweet girl?
    So close to life
    So full of pink peonies and gentle verve.

What would you say if I told you
    I wanted to be the nightmare you claim for your own?

ART
OF A
POET

♥

It's the art of a poet
    To take something unerringly ugly
    And give it the right words
    To make it something lovely

REMEMBERING

We watch the stars
  To pull down the blue ink
  In the wide bowl of the sky
  And use it to write philosophies
  About the universe beyond the curved slope of our horizons
  Because sometimes
  The dark abyss of the unknown
  Is less lonely and less terrifying than our own remembering

OUT MY DOOR

What a self-fulfilling prophecy it is
　　To pave a yellow brick road
　　Line it with exit signs
　　Protect its boundaries with monsters
　　And then grieve when people inevitably walk
　　Down that path
　　And out my door

THE BOMB

The bomb in my chest
    Ticks louder
    Each day
    Counting
    Down
    To
    A
    Time
    Where
    I will self-detonate
    And implode

If only there were gentle hands
    To reach inside the chamber of my chest
    Cradle my ticking heart
    And bravely turn it off.

NEVER
FORGET

♥

She wore black
    And coloured in her many scars
    With red sharpie
    Like fresh blood against the ancient wounds
    She wanted to remember every hurt
    Illustrate every painful memory
    As a warning to everyone
    And herself
    That she would never forget

LEGACY
OF MEN

♥

This is a story of boy meets evil
    With the face of an angel
    And a body that could tempt a saint to sin

Of a time before the boy became a man
    When he met the demon
    By the name
    Of
    Delilah
    And spoke her title in a breath of supplication

This is the journey of that boy
    From the sweet stumble over lust
    To the willing jump he made
    Thinking he would land in
    Love's perfumed embrace

This is the story of what happens
    When the boy lands on the spikes of cruelty
    Savagely impaled by lies
    Where he brutally bleeds out

This is the story of what a woman
    Will do
    For
    Revenge

The legacy of men.

YOU & ME

Sometimes
    I yearn for the apocalypse
    So that all the nonsense will implode
    And the only things left
    Are you
    And
    me

PRETTY FISH

You were born a pretty fish
   Put into a pretty bowl
   To swim around looking pretty
   For the rest of eternity
   What would happen if the glass smashed?
   Would you grow lungs and legs
   Deformed, but free?
   Or die
   So pretty
   In the glistening glass?

STRONGER
FOR IT

♥

I was born in a stinking mire
   But I made it into compost
   Took sustenance from the refuse and rooted in the soil

It was on the filth of my mistakes
   That I rose to the greatest of heights
   And I was all the stronger for it

FORGED
FROM FIRE

If you succumb to the heat
    You will melt to your core
    And nothing is ever as strong as something
    Forged from fire.

WITCH, BITCH, QUEEN

♥

She was a witch, a bitch and a cold-hearted queen.

She was a witch
 Made of magic I wanted to shape in my hands
 A force so great I shuddered at her power
 And reverently learned the shape of each spell
 So I might wield her.

She was a bitch
 More magnificent than any woman I had ever met
 Because she liked her world cold and anti-septic clean.
 They judged her for that and her words
 The way they hit their targets
 Precisely
 Rat tat tat
 A semi-automatic weapon with a chamber of red lips.

She was a cold-hearted queen
    Who ruled without aid from a throne she made herself
    In a kingdom of steel towers and glass ceilings
    That she punctured with the lance of her ambition
    And watched crumble to dust beneath her stiletto heels

She was a witch, a bitch, and a cold-hearted queen.
    Sticks and stones would never break her bones.

    (It was easier to hate her than submit an application to be
    loved by her)

WITCHCRAFT
OF
WOMANHOOD

♥

The witchcraft of womanhood

I sipped from the chalice
    Sweet moonlight down my throat
    Silky and silver as the ribbon of water
    Sewn through the moss-covered ground
    At my bare feet

I danced over the green mottled earth
    Wet mud sucking at my toes
    Packed earth vibrating with the kick drum beat
    Of the revellers circling the fire
    At my naked side

Women revolve around the flames
 Leaping through the sparks
 They chant in one voice like an echo
 That emanates from the earth

HOWL
OF
WOLVES

The howl of wolves
 In the dark bowl of night
 Echoes eerie
 Like a gong struck in my chest
 They call to me
 And naturally
 I follow

A GIRL
IS A
WEAPON

A girl is a weapon
    Whether or not she knows how to wield her power
    Is another question entirely

I CAN GIVE YOU (YOU)

♥

I don't want to give you the world.

I can't afford a diamond ring or a house so high on a hill.

I can't take you on a trip or pay your way through school.

But...

I can give you something I've been aching to give
    Since I first saw you so confused on my stoop
    A child without a dream
    You see,
    I can give you *you*.

LOVE OF YOUR LIFE (YOU)

Let the love of your life be the woman looking back at you in the mirror.

She is your best friend forever and your tireless champion,
If only you'll give her words to speak and the power to be
Seen.

MISTAKE

Sometimes the only lesson you learn
  Is from a mistake
  Not worth making again.

DREAMS
ON FIRE

You can't light a fire without kindling.

The scraps and waste of life that didn't work out
    That tore strips off your soul
    And ripped through your defences?

Those are your tinder to light your dreams on fire.

THE WEIGHT OF LOVE

♥

I love with my whole soul
    But the weight of that love is too much for some.

They drop it in the dirt.
    Trip over it as they run away.

One day,
    I hope I find someone Atlas strong enough
    To hold it up.

YOU BROKE HER

You broke her.

So I took her and taught her how to fill her cracks with gold.

DANGEROUS LOVE

♥

She is tangled up in his dangerous love
    Wrapped in the yarn of his malicious lies
    Like a fly trapped in a cotton web

I want to be the shears that cut her free

24/7 DINER

♥

I'm a night person
    Because she works at the 24/7 diner
    Off exist 99
    I'm a pie person too
    Because it's the only edible thing they serve

SINK
OR SWIM

♥

She was deep dark waters
    And I was never taught how to swim

I was afraid of her sharks and currents
    The absolute blackness at her depth

But as I watched
    She tossed and churned
    Eternally turbulent and ill at ease

So, I took the chance to soothe her peaks
    And dove right in head first.

Love is sink or swim.

SURVIVE
YOUR LOVE

♥

Who told you
　　You were hard to love
　　And what made you
　　Think that was a horrible thing?
　　Everything hard is worth having
　　We spend our entire lives
　　Doing the hard things to survive
　　I will tell you now
　　I can survive your love
　　And I want to

NIGHTMARE
SLAYER

What makes you tremble
   Alone in the dark
   What is the stuff of the nightmares
   You imagine at midnight
   Let me know all those things you fear
   So that I might slay them
   Even while you dream

BREAK MY OWN HEART

♥

I would break my own heart a million times over
    If it meant keeping you safe
    From a million heartbreaks of your own

COME ALIVE

She was a live wire I wanted to hold in my hands
    Take her electricity between my teeth
    And feel her currents race along my skin

She was the shock I needed to come alive

UP IN FLAMES

Touch me
    And
    I burn
    A lit match to dry timber
    The press of your lips on my skin
    Douses me like amber liquor
    And up I go
    In flames

BABY GIRL

♥

Baby girl
    Don't think
    I'll forget that beneath the sting
    Of angry bees
    You taste as sweet as honey

LIKE A PEARL

♥

Her beauty lay
    Within her brain
    Like a pearl trapped
    Between layers of pink velvet
    I thought I needed
    Currency
    To buy it
    Class
    To own it
    But I realized the only way
    To gain a pearl
    Like her
    Was to be gifted it

TOO LONG/
TOO OFTEN

♥

I'm sorry if I kiss you too much

    Too long

    And

    Too often

    But I know the time will come

    Where you won't want my touch at all

    And so

    I take advantage

    Of your lips

    And that smile against my smile

    Because when it is gone

    I fear my mouth will forget the shape of yours

    And the taste of yours

    Even though my heart with forever mourn

WAITING
FOR YOU

♥

You went to hell
    On a one-way ticket
    Condemned and beaten
    Only to meet Satan amid the flames
    He took your warm hand, kissed your fingers with cold lips
    And said,
    "I've been waiting for you."

LIGHT & DARK WOMAN

♥

She was conceived, born, and raised in the light
    The dark, they told her, was full of horrors
    If she stayed far away from the shadows
    She would thrive

So why did they whisper to her like lovers do
    A caress at the base of her sensitive spine
    A sinful kiss of desire at her neck
    Rage tucked like flaming tissue around her
    Strange multifaceted heart?

Because nothing is all black or all white.

MADE
TO BE
BROKEN

I fell into the deep abyss
    Between the mountains
    Of love and hate
    Arms pinned
    Heartbeat shallow
    Mind awash with the fear that this was my new and bitter forever
    It was not comfortable but there was some safety
    In being alone in the dark
    With no one to hurt me but myself

I tried to work myself out of the pit of despair
    But it was hard to remember
    the heart was made to be broken and the only one who could
    mend it
    was me

INNER BEAUTY

♥

She was an old coat
    With pink silk lining
    A cracked vase filled with
    Passion red roses
    A hundred-dollar bill
    Found in a forgotten purse

She surprised you with her beauty
    And instead of judging you for your shock
    She blessed you with her kindness
    Instead

DADDY ISSUES

♥

She had daddy issues.

She wore these problems
    Shame-faced but bold
    Like a tattoo that seemed
    A good idea
    While drunk.

I won't lie.
    They drew me to her
    Those daddy issues
    But not for the reasons you think.

It was a call to action
    For a man like me
    To show the woman what she could be
    If she had a man to love and protect her
    While she fixed her problems herself

A GUN
OR PEN?

♥

What is more dangerous?
    A man with a gun
    Or one posed with a pen?

The kind who threatens your safety
    The one where you might end up dead

Or the one that will never let you go
    Who will trap you forever with that pen
    And his ink
    In a poem.

KILL YOU
OR KISS YOU

♥

You can call me beautiful
    Compare me to a summer's day
    Or a spring morning
    Romanticize my winter storms
    Into cleansing tempest that stir your soul

But we both know just like the
    Mother nature
    You compare me too
    I am so much more than that

My summer's day could scorch you up
    My spring morning could leave you blind
    And my winter storms could rip you apart like confetti

I could as easily kill you as kiss you.

DAMAGED
SOULS

♥

Damaged souls
    Aren't broken irrevocably.

They have a condition;
    PTSD.

After wars of the heart blew open their ribs and scored shrapnel
into flesh,
    They dream about the horrors of battle
    Stare at the scars that will never fade
    And feel the ones on their soul that will never be seen.

The magic of healing
>Is that such a small act
>Can make a lifetime of destruction seem small too
>Wrapped in your arms
>Washed clean by your faith
>Day by day
>My damaged soul is made once more whole.

WATER

♥

Be water
    Constantly moving
    Flowing through time and space
    Carrying the debris of the past
    But still
    Streaming
    Full of life

Do not let life
    Turn you into ice
    Trapping the detritus
    Like scars and puncture points
    In your cold soul
    Stopping you from ever
    Moving on
    Again

KINTSUGI

Fill the cracks and puncture wounds in your heart
    Inflicted by the callous acts of others
    With the mortar of self-love
    Kintsugi

IN A KISS

♥

He ripped her world apart with his bare hands
    Sucked out the poison and spit out the bones
    Until all that was left was
    Possibility and choice
    He handed back to her with his lips
    In a kiss.

BLEEDING HEARTS

(KING)

Definition: when the cards are played face up
and visible to all the players.

WHY POETRY?

♥

Someone once asked me,
   "Why poetry?"

And I said,
   "Why does the sea kiss the shore over and over like an eager lover
   With a salty tongue?
   Why does the moon reflect the sun turning golden rays into
   Silver fragments?
   And why does the bee visit the spring flowers
   A buffet of pastel blooms?
   Because it is only natural
   Because they are born with a purpose written in their code
   Just as mine is penned in prose."

POETRY

♥

Poetry gives words to feelings with no end
    A road map for the vast plains of the heart
    A lighthouse for those lost in its inky depths
    And an oasis for those wandering its desserts parched with thirst.

IN MY POETRY

♥

I hide you in my poetry
    As unsubtle as a gun beneath a blanket.
    I want you to feel your spirit in the words
    Know that as I craft this prose
    It is you seeped in the ink
    You I feel moving my hand across the page
    And you in the beat of my heart as it times
    Each legato phrase.

SOUL IN
SCRIPT

♥

I don't want to text.

I want to press my fingers to the page and
    Smudge my print in the ink
    On the paper
    As I write you a love letter.
    My soul scrawled in script for you to decipher.

READER'S SOUL

The first time I read a book
    I found I had hooks in my heart
    Where the words could hang
    And ornament my soul.

I am a hoarder of language. A gorger of verbosity.

LOOK AT HER

"Look at her," I whisper.

"Look at the way she breaths like a tsunami pulling a tidal range of energy in through her parted lips."

"Look at the way she moves like her muscles are tied to the rhythm of a song only she can discern."

"Look at the way she reads a book with her finger resting on the page like a cartographer mapping new lands."

"Look at her," I whisper. "Is it any wonder I stare?"

DEAD
LANGUAGE

♥

I was an old book
    None one picked up at the library
    To spread their fingers over my pages and
    Absorb my words

I was almost forgotten
    A dead language like Latin

Until the girl with the glasses
    Who dreamt of days long past
    Pulled me out of the dust
    Cracked open my spine
    And exposed my pages to her light

STRANGEST FICTION

♥

I read novels
  To live life
  While I waited for more
  I struck my hands between the books
  On the shelf at the library
  And waited
  For someone
  To take it in theirs
  To make with me
  A life more beautiful
  Than the strangest fiction

FIT TO ME

Fit to me
    Made for me
    Bone of my bone
    Broken
    Lost or freed
    You are a state of mine
    Eternal
    Bone
    Of my
    Bone

LAST KISS

That first kiss was a promise
    Sealed in the petal pink wax of your lips
    That my mouth
    Would be yours until
    Our very last kiss

DREAMS
LIKE PEARLS

Dreams shine like pearls in her eyes.
   I become an artist, a collector; stringing salt water gems on
   necklaces
That she may wear around her throat.

SECRET IN HER SMILE

♥

A secret in her smile
    Tucked in a rosy furl
    I want to pull it out with my teeth
    Soothe the paper cut with my tongue
    Dip in the well of her blood and write
    My own secret on her lips
    So that every time she speaks
    Every lick of those lips
    And drag of breath through her mouth
    She feels me
    Her tongue scraps the scar of my secret on
    The inside of her pout
    And she can't deny the truth of it
    Of me
    Of us
    I've branded her with it
    She's mine

KISS TO A ROSE

I pressed a kiss to the center of a rose
    It twisted
    Unfurled
    Dew in its folds
    Sweet on my lips
    Cool against my tongue
    I suck at the fragile bloom
    And feel like
    God
    As it blossoms under my touch

AMBER EYES

Her amber eyes trapped every tragedy of her past in the dark flecks and inconsistent whorls of brighter gold. I knew if I took my time, I could read her story in them as eloquently as hearing it from her lips.

TOO MUCH HEAVEN

She was too much heaven
   And I everything hell
   We met clandestinely
   At the kiss of dawn
   And the death of day
   It was forbidden to connect
   Because together we would have made
   A heaven of hell
   And a hell of heaven
   And where is the sense in that?

There are no rules in love.

DEADLY
BEAUTIFUL

♥

She was gorgeous
    Like the edge of a sharp blade in the light
    Striking as a flint against rock
    As deadly to my heart
    As an arrow tipped in poison punctured through
    My chest

THE DREAM OF YOU

I woke up to the sight of you
  Dawn sluiced across your skin like gold
  And for the first time
  In a long time
  The dream of you was not a nightmare
  Because my reality matched the fantasy

I FOUND LOVE

♥

I found love when I was eight
    Pressed petals the colour of blood
    Hidden between the pages
    Of a book I was too young to read

Again,
    At that awkward time
    When my voice lacked depth
    Then suddenly
    Fell to the bottom of a well
    That signalled maturity and I thought
    "Finally, I am old enough to love."

But by fifteen, I had seen only wraiths,
    Lust like brass when I would have gold
    Infatuation thin as gauze and just as easily torn

At eighteen,
    My half-formed soul felt fallow
    My dreams withered to husks and tumble weeds
    I was old enough for first love, they said
    But my heart yearned for that and more

They couldn't have known what would happen
    That same year
    When I saw you across a parking lot
    How my heart would age a decade with each beat
    And the hollow cage of my chest would be at once so filled

In a second, I was found.
    Too young, too old, too every single thing at once
    Because with you I was made and unmade
    Everything was possible because of you
    Yet nothing was necessary
    Because my ten-year journey
    For the other half of my soul
    Was done.
    And that was all I ever wanted.

YOUR VOICE

♥

Your voice is between the lines, my queen
    Echoed in the white before the black
    It is the swell of words that rest
    Behind the apex of my throat

Your scent is caught between my teeth
    Sinks among the grooves there and gives them taste
    Of clouds
    Dew upon my palate
    I hide you under my tongue

Your body walks my lines at night
    It warms the skin beneath my arms
    Settles against my chest
    A thumb in the hollow of my collarbone
    It whispers your breath into mine

Your heart rests in the gaps
  Between my ribs
  It sits and breathes my breath
  It webs the links between my toes
  And when I swim, my queen, it is on you I float

SWEET
STONE FRUIT

♥

She was sun-warmed
> The skin behind her ear like ripe summer fruit
> A peach split open on wet grass
> I wondered
> If I pressed my lips to the crease between her thighs
> Would she still smell of sweet stone fruit?

LIVING IN
SIN WITH YOU

❤

I would fall from grace
   Again and again
   If it meant living in sin
   With you

I GET LOST

The woman I love has eyes like the forest floor
    Dappled in golden daylight, dark with evergreens and light
    with spring frost.
    I get lost in the treed twilight of that gaze
    And don't care to ever be found.

THEY SAY

They say
> You are too bold
> Your smile so wide it could swallow
> The world

They say
> You are too strong
> When atlas is the man who holds up
> The world
> And you are only a girl

They say
> You should mind your place
> In the kitchen or the bedroom
> Outside the home beside your man
> You are his accessory

They say
    These things
    Because
    If they let you shine
    You would blind them all with your light

I say
    I would live the rest of my life without sight
    If it meant feeling the warmth of your glow
    Every day until I die

HER LAUGH

♥

Her laugh reminded me
    Of the *pop*
    When the cork escapes champagne
    And effervescence spills over my hands
    Bubbling with joy

I want to drink her laugh down every day

I GOT YOU

When the world comes for you

When it tears at you with vicious teeth and cracks open your bones
to eat out the marrow
    Mercilessly aimed at your destruction

I got you

When the villains come as they do
    In every shape and size
    Masquerading as friends or announcing themselves as foe

I got you

When there is danger
    A sword swinging at your head or a lance aimed at your heart
    A bullet ready to pierce your armour and obliterate your
    priceless life

I got you

LIKE ORIGAMI

❤

Bent and folded
    Like origami
    Into the shape of my desires
    I craft you as art and paint you in the red colours of my lust.

DARKER

♥

You want it harder
   Darker
   So long it hurts

You want it with a sinner
   A bad boy
   A man without a plan

You want it the way they tell you not to
   The way the villain likes it
   The way the harlot has it

I want it darker too
   Harder
   So long it hurts

Sometimes love
    Isn't sugar and sweetness
    And everything fine

Sometimes love
    Is rough bites and deep moans
    And making you mine

LOVE YOU HARD

♥

I want to love you hard
    Fill all your holes with my fingers
    Stop you up at every puncture point
    Give you my every breath to breathe
    So that you are full up with your love of me
    And you will never yearn for anything else again

LIKE A GLUTTON

Pinned to the mattress like a butterfly by the wings
  I run my fingers
  Down
  Her soft, vibrant body
  Dig them
  Into the tender places
  That make her keen into my mouth
  I eat her moans
  Like a glutton
  And fill her with my love in return

LITTLE MISS

You wouldn't think
    Such a little miss
    Could yell so loud at night
    With her ankles bound
    And her hands chained
    To the headboard
    Banging against the wall

You wouldn't think
    Such a little miss
    Would make a big guy like me bend
    But while she may be the one tied up
    I am the one she has wrapped up tight
    Around the crook of her little finger

LOVE
DARKLY

I loved her darkly,
    And I didn't care if that damned me to Hell
    So long as I could rule there with her.

WHAT LOVE IS

And looking at her in that moment

—The setting sun gilding her face like a Klimt painting as she smiled demurely out the window, blood on her delicate fingers, my gold at her long throat—

I finally understood what love was.

DIVINE KISS

♥

I look at you
    And suddenly
    I believe in magic
    And mythological beings with wings
    Who reign over heaven
    And only fall to earth
    When they find a man
    Worthy
    Of their divine kiss

TWO HALVES

♥

What if ancient things are true
    What if we were once born
    With four arms
    Four legs
    Four eyes
    And two hearts
    But the Gods feared the power of that force
    Of one complete soul
    And broke us with a lightning strike
    In half
    Now when we are born
    We wander and are lost
    Until we find the person
    We were split from
    At birth
    And become once more
    Whole.

I LOVE YOU

"I love you."

Isn't it incredible
    That one phrase can be
    A truth, a lie, and a weapon?

I FALL

I fall
   I fall
   I fall

And it is your choice where I land.

She loves me. She loves me not.

FOREVER
SPINNING

I never liked to dance until we started to tip toe
    Around each other
    Waltzing through the halls in time with one another
    We tapped out a repartee that said
    We didn't care
    But the spin of our hard shoes against the ground
    Entangled like ballerinas in a Russian music box
    Forever spinning as one
    Said differently

LANGUAGE OF DESIRE

♥

The language of desire
    Is the tracks of red worn down the back
    All roads leading to sin

It's the colour of her sex
    As it blushes blossom pink
    And unfurls like the blooms in spring

It's the slope of the valley between her breasts
    Brushed in dew like dawn over the hills
    And the sigh from her lips
    Breaking against mine
    Like the waves against the rocks

The language of desire
 Is written here
 Between two bodies in the dark
 But I find it often as I walk the earth
 Between the flowers and the glades
 And I'm reminded again
 As I often am
 That desire is a natural thing

LOVE
LANGUAGE

♥

She is written in a language I don't understand
    Something dead and ancient
    With hard consonants where there should be
    Soft vowels
    I want to spend the rest of my life
    Learning to be fluent

Love is bilingual.

A TASTE
FOR HER

I had a taste for her
    The wet between her thighs like salted pasta water
    The skin behind her knees smooth as a plum beneath my teeth
    If I pierce it with my teeth I could break her open
    And drink her right up

I was an epicure at a feast of delicacies

LIKE THE SEA

She is like the sea
    Just because she chooses to kiss you
    Again and again
    Sweetly lapping at the shore of your boundaries
    Do not forget
    Like the sea
    She could swallow you whole

SHE THE SEA

♥

She tastes like fresh brine
  Like sea water

I'll ride her in softly
  Rocking
  Like an incoming tide

And even when she ebbs after the crest
  I know she'll flow back to me again

The sea always returns to kiss the shore.

I THOUGHT
OF HER

♥

I thought of her
  In the dark folds of night
  Between the pages of the sun's set and rise
  I thought of her in the midnight hours
  With my fist around my flesh
  Until I spilled like moonlight across my chest

RELIGION
OF OUR
LOVE

♥

The last time I prayed
    It was at the altar of her sex
    I dipped my finger in the holy waters
    Anointed my tongue and baptized my lips
    Until I was pure and made whole
    By the religion of our love

THE WOMAN

♥

She was small
    But her heart was so large
    I could see it behind her eyes
    She made me feel ten feet tall and
    Strong enough to move the world
    How such a little thing could have powers
    So immense
    I'll never know
    Mostly because
    She will never tell

The secret power of the woman behind the man.

READ ME

❤

He folded my legs back
  Like two halves of a book open for him to read
  ~~Not to read~~
  To venerate
  To dedicate to memory so that
  He could recite the taste of me
  The smell of me
  Anytime he wanted

ACT OF GOD

They say you need an act of God to find a miracle
  I found mine pressed between her lips
  When she smiled

LIFE'S
PURPOSE

♥

In whatever planes of existence there are
    On any star or parallel planet
    You and I are together
    Infinitely
    Inevitably
    Because nothing makes sense
    In any language or any place
    Without our love to decode life's purpose

NIGHTLIGHT

You are a light that never goes out, no matter how dark my world becomes.

Nightlight.

VELVET LOVE

She took my strained silence
    And turned it to velvet
    Wound the soft edges around my jagged soul
    And swaddled me in the comfort of her love.

BRING ME
PEACE

♥

You bring me peace
  By inciting madness
  Because nothing feels so big
  So hard and unendurable
  When chaos reigns beside you

HER

What a simple question it is
    To ask what brings me the most joy.

Some may say there is no simple answer
    But my response will always be:

Her.
    Today, tomorrow, and yesterday.

Under the awning of the bookstore
    When I kissed her ink stained fingers.

In the sheets of our bed before the dawn
    Is even a thought on the horizon
    With her face
    Tucked under my arm like a sleeping swan

Beside the garage where the scent of tar
    And gasoline is strong
    But all I can smell is the apple
    And sunshine scent of
    Her.

LEASE ON HAPPINESS

❤

You are more than the reason behind one smile.

You own the lease on my happiness.

LION-HEARTED GIRL

♥

Lion-hearted girl
    Who taught you to mute your roar
    Who took you to the zoo and told you that is where the lions
roam?

When in truth it is the lioness
    Who hunts down their prey
    Who feeds their young
    And protects the king of their jungle

So what does that make you, lion girl?

Queen of them all.

LOVE'S DUALITY

♥

Is it any wonder there are so many lovers
    Between May and December?

That the yin of fresh morning hours and heady new flowers
    Would fit with the yang of twilight evenings and seasoned
    feelings
    That someone so much younger could blossom under the
    authority
    Of someone with real maturity

Love's duality.

HUSH

When I tell you to
    Hush
    It is not because
    I don't love the sound
    Of your voice around the words
    You want to say
    Or the brain behind the power
    To say them

I tell you to
    Hush
    Because you have a sharp tongue
    To service your angry eyes
    But a tender heart
    That bruises after you
    Weaponize your words

I tell you to
    hush
    When you say my name
    Like a benediction
    Or a prayer
    Because I've read the desire
    In your body
    More eloquent than any words said

I tell you, my darling,
    To
    Hush
    Because I know you
    Not because I want to stop you
    Because I am proud of the knowing
    And I love showing
    Just how much I care

HALF HEAVEN/
HALF HELL

♥

She was half heaven half hell
    And each met at the apex of her thighs.
    When I worshiped there
    It was both a prayer and a sin.

SHE WAS
A QUEEN

♥

She was a queen
    Raised to sit on a golden throne
    In a kingdom of crystal and ice

All I had to offer was my sword of smoke and world of gasoline
    With soldiers shielded by leather and coated in tatts

My currency was love and loyalty
    In a market that traded in diamonds and class

I would do anything to convince her
    That she might have been raised to sit on a golden throne
    But she belonged on the seat of iron with a crown of steel
    At my side

WHAT I LOVE

♥

I found what I loved.

I was lucky
    Because I know many don't
    So while I wasn't exactly happy to do it
    —To leave—
    I knew I had found what I loved
    And I was happy to let them kill me for it.

A PUZZLE

I've been making a puzzle my entire life
    Exchanging pieces of my heart
    With pieces from other's souls
    The trick is
    —When they inevitably leave you—
    To make a puzzle
    That's missing
    It's portions

HEAVEN ON EARTH

♥

Those with certain faiths know
    That life is to be endured
    Ruled by psalms and bibles
    A sentence well served

So when the time comes to die
    You will be blessed in heaven
    And not cursed to bowls of a dire hell

Only, you are my heaven on earth
    And the only hell I will ever know is
    Life or death without you

THE
ASTRONOMY
OF YOU

♥

You are not perfect
    But
    I want to kiss each imperfection
    Like a constellation of freckles
    On your skin
    Connect the dots between them
    Until they are fully understood
    And remember
    That I have the privilege of knowing
    What so many others
    Have wished they could

An astronomist; I stare and wonder.

DIRTY POETRY

Dirty Poetry.

I admit
    I love
    The crest of your hips against mine
    The way your feet cross like a bow tied around my back

But I feel no shame in saying
    It is the way I breathe words into your neck
    And feel them sink into your skin
    Floating through your head
    Until you moan them back
    That makes me come

Because there is no greater high
    Than fucking your mind.

HONEY BEAR

Wet leaked from her sex
    Like an overturned jar
    Of honey
    I was a bear
    A beast
    It was in my nature
    To crouch between her legs
    Dip my fingers in the nectar
    And feast until the jar ran
    Dry

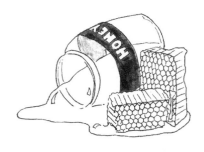

NEVER STOP
LOVING YOU

♥

Will you finally trust me
    If I promise never to leave
    If even
    When I die
    I vow to return
    To ghost beside you as you live on
    To haunt you gently through the days
    To protect you like a poltergeist in violent bursts of energy
    To dismiss St. Peter's pearly gates
    So that I may continue my heaven with you
    Even if I cannot touch you
    Talk to you
    Press the kisses you like to the backs of your hands
    I will eschew it all
    If it means finally
    You'll trust me

I'll never stop loving you.

226

ROUGH LOVE

I wanted a rough love
    A tough love
    An 'I would fight for you' love
    A demonic possession kinda love That fills you up to the brim
    So nothing else exists and you almost
    —but not quite—
    Forget yourself

The love people think you can
    Exorcise
    The love priests condemn
    That makes angels plummet
    Straight through earth
    Into the sweltering embrace of hell
    Because some things are even lovelier
    In the dark

Black is my favourite colour.

OLD LADY

Do you know why a biker calls his woman
   Old Lady?
   Because he knows that he will still love her
   When their romance is old and their hair is gray
   Because he knows the only thing that will change
   With time
   Is that every day
   He will grow to love her more

KINDNESS

I want to teach my sons
    That the only kind of man
    They should aspire to be
    Is the human
    Who is kind to every being.

IF I GO

♥

If I go
    And do not return
    You must know
    That I wear you forever in my side
    A broken rib that beats with its own pulse
    Like a second heart in my chest
    A piece of you inside me
    I would never return
    Not even to heal myself of the pain
    That comes from knowing
    You might never be mine again

WHEN I DIE

When I die
    I want to do it
    With your love like celestial dust
    In my veins
    So when my body turns to ash
    My soul will soar
    And our love will be eternalized
    In the stars

WHEN I'M
GONE

♥

When I'm gone

Here are the things I want you to know:

I want you to know the first time I saw you,
    I felt the shape of my heart in my chest
    The weight of each beat, the heat of each churning chamber.
    It all came alive as I looked at you and
    Knew
    My heart was never mine to own.
    It had always been lost and yours
    And in that moment, it was found.

I want you to know the first time we kissed
　　My toes curled and my mind went blank
　　Pure, blissful meditation in physical manifestation
　　The taste on your tongue was honey
　　Pressed between my teeth
　　And I knew
　　I would kiss you for the rest of my life if I could
　　And now,
　　I know I did.

I want you to know that sex with you
　　Was so much more than fingers and tongues
　　The flutter of our lids
　　That I prayed between your parted thighs
　　And worshiped at the twin temples of your breast
　　The way a votary does for his God
　　And I knew
　　I would always be your zealot
　　Patient and enduring
　　Fervent to the point of sin.

I want you to know when I am gone
　　That you gave me the greatest gift a person can
　　You gifted me your heart
　　But you also gave me mine
　　Through the prism of your love
　　I found the meaning of my life.

CHROME
QUEEN

♥

Just remember in those moments when I am not there
    That my life changed the moment I saw you.
    A parking lot became a kingdom
    For an asphalt ruler of bikes and men
    And his chrome queen who reigned over them all.

THE KING
IS DEAD

♥

When the King dies
    The revolution begins

They had no choice to go to war
    Brother against brother

Because the king was dead
    The kingdom was fractured
    And there was no him left to hold it together.

WIDOW
(CRESSIDA)

Definition: also referred to as a blind.
Hand of cards placed face down on the table
so that they are not visible tothe players.

GODDAMN
THE QUEEN

♥

The king is dead
   Goddamn the queen.

NO GOODBYE

♥

You never said goodbye.

    And you always did before.

    At the door to our house before work with a kiss I felt in my toes.

You never said goodbye

    And you promised me you would

    When the day came that we went to sleep holding hands

    Knowing

    That we would not wake up again.

You never said goodbye

    And now I can't help feeling

    That this isn't a goodbye for good.

That one day when I am sitting in the kitchen
    You will come in carrying apples and tell me to
    Bake you a pie like I did that very first day we were in love
    I'll have flour in my hair and juice on my cheek
    That you'll lick off with laughing lips
    And everything will have been
    As it was before
    When you were still here.

NO PRINCE CHARMING

♥

He was no Prince Charming
    On a white steed galloping with the wind
    In his golden hair

Oh, he had a ride under his thighs
    Made of iron and chrome
    And a kingdom at his command
    Made of rebels and ruffians

But he was no story book hero

He was my real-life knight in leather on his beast of metal
    And he was coming for me

TOO YOUNG

He was too young, too wild and reckless, filled to the brim with sex and vigor.

His eyes promised to burn me alive, incinerate my inhibitions, char my morals into ash and my soul into tinder.

He held the torch, the threat against everything I had ever stood for, and he had the audacity to tell me to *come closer*.

Yet, I found myself obeying.

Willingly, I lay myself on the pyre at his feet with open arms.

Because if I was going to burn, I was going to make sure we did it together.

TREE IN
A STORM

♥

I was a storm of calamity
    Cast adrift on a sea of black doings
    And loosely drawn rebel rules

He was an old growth oak
    With roots sunk deep in the earth
    Limbs stretching wide across the sky
    Standing sentry across centuries
    As the world toiled away beneath its leaves

I could whip around that kind of man
    Cause hurricanes with my spirit
    Quake the earth with my tempers
    But he would remain forever unmoved
    Standing tall and strong and free

I think that's why I liked him.

UNTIL I
MET YOU

♥

I didn't know how much was enough
  Until I met you
  And never again thought to ask for more

EACH TIME
WE TOUCH

♥

Each time you touch me, I fall to pieces. Fragments of my soul scattered all over the floor. But I know you will kneel amongst the carnage and piece me back together fraction by fraction like a tactile mathematician until I am whole once more but changed for the better by the texture of your hands on my soul.

TRUE
FRIENDSHIP

♥

You were everything I aspired to be
    Tall and strong like an oak
    Flourishing with burnished leaves
    The colour of your eyes
    I grew around you like a vine
    Seeking your heat and light
    Because without you I would wither
    Even if I would not die
    And after a few years of carrying
    My weight
    You encouraged me to more
    And when I grew my own roots
    We stood together in the earth
    Together 'til we died

The nature of true friendship.

DEMANDS
OF THE
FLESH

I don't need romance
    In candy hearts and roses

I need romance
    In my back against a tree
    Skirt rucked up by a strong hand
    The other spreading my knees

I need the love of your body
    Not in cheek kisses and holding hands

I need your body
    To meet my sinful flesh's greedy demands

PET ME

Like a cat
    I'll purr
    If you pet me
    Just right

But like a cat
    If you cross me
    I'll gauge your eyes out
    With my claws

WORDS
UNDER THE
SKIN

♥

He read things I didn't know
    I had written under the surface
    With his hands skimming my edges
    And cupping my folds
    Reading the words I was never able to say
    Like a blind man with braille etched into my skin

MY
APOCALYPSE

♥

You are all four horsemen of my apocalypse.

I could taste my destruction on your lips
   But it was sweeter than wild flower honey
   And so, I drank it down.

When the end came, all I smelled was flowers.

FALL FROM
GRACE

♥

He was my apple, my serpent, and my Satan.
My ultimate fall from grace.

What if Eve desired to leave Eden all along?

YOU WERE GONE

♥

Then you were gone
    And there were a million different ways
    I hadn't loved you yet
    A thousand other ways I could have told you
    Those words
    Hundreds of moments I could have spent
    With you instead
    And then in only one moment
    You were gone
    And there would be no more time left with you
    Because where you went
    I couldn't follow

GRACELESS QUEEN

♥

I feel the loss of you heavy like a mantle over my shoulders
Dragging across the ground with every leaden step
I wear the crown of mourning without poise
A graceless Queen.

ASK & ANSWER

♥

If I answer your questions
    Your
    "how are yous"
    And
    "what's ups"
    If I open my mouth to respond
    I'll cry
    And that is not what you asked for

If it is
    If you are truly worried about the tragedy
    Folded into the creases beside my eyes like prayers '
    In Israel's Western Wall
    And the pallor of pain blasted onto my cheeks
    Like La Melancholia
    All you have to do
    Is ask

The right
Questions
And prepare to hold me while
I break

I SURVIVED

I survived
    I am no longer nice
    Sweet, pink, and new
    But
    I am not cruel
    And that is all you should ask for.

HE WAS

♥

He was ink stained hands
    And grease smeared jeans
    That fit just right

He was apple orchards in the fall
    And motorcycle rides
    With the sea wind in his hair

He was uncharted wilderness
    King of a realm without rules
    And I was the one he wanted there
    at his side

HE IS
NOT DEAD

♥

He is not dead.
> I love him and I wear him in my heart.
> So.
> He is not dead.
> I know him and I live out his days in my head.
> So.
> He is not dead.
> I am still alive but half-formed because he is not here also.
> So.
> He is not dead.
> Because if he was, I would be too.
> *The stages of grief: denial.*

ACKNOWLEDGEMENTS

Poetry is one of the most difficult forms of writing because it follows no set rules and its very fluidity is mean to be questioned and interpreted differently by each reader. Maybe it's for this reason that I've always been drawn to it, the rebel in me yearns to break the rules and rewrite hard to understand truths into easily digestible sound bites. It might be the reason I have never, ever thought to call myself a poet even though I've been writing poems since I was a teen. Truthfully, even after publishing this work of poems, I will prob-ably still refrain from usually the epitaph in conjunction with myself. What makes a poet? As with most titles, part of me believes it should be designated by a certificate or the complete of a program, bestowed upon me by the Queen of England like a knighthood or blessed unto me by a priest. But the truth is, love and life make a poet of everyone, even if the words are only felt in our hearts and the rhythms only echoed in the beat of our pulses. We feel so deeply as human beings, I think it's a natural inclination to desire to put words to those emotions, and what-ever words you give them are poetry by nature because every emotion is beautiful and well felt.

So, I supposed I could call myself a poet just as easily as I do others, but whether or not I do, I hope you enjoyed this collection of poems. I wrote them from the perceptive of a man, both because I have always identified in strange and intimate way with the opposite sex, but also because ostensibly, the narrator of this book is King Kyle Garro from my novels, Lessons in Corruption and After The Fall. King is my poet biker, a man who grew up in motorcycle boots with a convicted felon as a father with the forecourt of a garage as his backyard. He is not the type of man who would ever assume would have romance and empathy in his soul, which is exactly the reason he is one of the most beautiful characters I have ever written. Some of these poems are featured in Lessons in Corruption and his subsequent book After the Fall, but most are original to the collection. They tell the story of his life and love from both novels, but they also tell the greater story of someone who is inherently misunder-stood because of their origins and who struggles to define himself outside of social mores. King uses his poetry to rewrite himself, just as I think everyone who gives voice to their emotions can rewrite the trajectory of their thoughts and life.

Now, on to thanking the many people who encouraged me to pursue this project.

Thank you Allaa for going on this journey with me. You read every poem almost as soon as it was written; read them and critiqued them until they were polished as perfectly as the pearls we love. You hold my hand through everything I go through both personally and professionally and even though we live on different continents across the world from each other, I feel the echo of your beautiful presence every day of my life and it brings me untold comfort and joy.

Ella, my love, you are one of the best friends I've ever had and I love your face, your gentle voice, and your blunt, beautiful way.

To Ali Silver, my immensely talented illustrator. You read my words and spun them into visual gold. I can't tell you what it means to me to do this project with one of my lifelong best friends and with an artist I have always admired.

Armie Armstrong, the female love of my life, thank you for listening to my creative deluge whenever I get an idea, good or bad.

Michelle Clay, how do I count the myriad of ways you love and support me? I can't. I feel you like a warmth at my back whenever I doubt myself. Thank you for reading my words and for always identifying with them. The poem 'Hush' is for you.

Annette, thank you for being there for me whenever I need you. Your presence in my life has calmed my frenetic worth life and your kindness has soothed my soul.

Fiona—Petunia, Feefers, Fifi, Matherton, Mathy— the nature of true friendship is about you. I was such a shy, soft, overly sensitive thing when we met and you were this confident, fun, and kind light I was drawn toward. I've learned so much from you over the years about being a good friend and a good woman. I'll never be able to thank you for the beauty and longevity of our friendship except by reciprocating that goodness until the day we die.

Lauren, you are the kindest, softest, prettiest heart I know. I feel so lucky to have you back in my life in such a profound way. Even just the thought of you makes me smile.

To my boys, you've taught me so much about men over the

years—both good and bad. I wouldn't be me without the seven of you informing my preteen, teen, and early adult years. You shaped me, you ground me, and you love me no matter what. It feels like having a super power to know I have incredible men like you at my back.

To the poets who have influenced me over the years; e.e cummings, Maya Angelou, Lord Byron, Percy Shelley, John Keats, Pablo Neruda, William Shakespeare, John Milton, Dante, Atticus, Lang Leav, Amanda Lovelace, Michael Faudet, Nikita

Gill, Tyler Knott Gregson, Beau Taplin, and Rupi Kaur... and so many more I cannot list them.

Finally, to the love of my life. Every love poem I have ever written is inspired by you because my heart has and always will be owned by you. I feel you every day in the vessels and cham-bers of my heart as it beats. I cannot wait to love you forever.

MORE BOOKS BY
GIANA DARLING

THE EVOLUTION OF SIN TRILOGY

The Affair

The Secret

The Consequence

THE FALLEN MEN SERIES

Lessons in Corruption

Welcome to the Dark Side

Good Gone Bad

After the Fall

THE ENSLAVED DUET

Enthralled

Enamoured

THE ELITE SEVEN SERIES

Sloth

ABOUT
GIANA DARLING

Giana Darling is a *USA Today*, *Wall Street Journal*, and Top 40 Best Selling Canadian romance writer who specializes in the taboo and angsty side of love and romance. She currently lives in beautiful British Columbia where she spends time riding on the back of her man's bike, baking pies, and reading snuggled up with her cat Persephone.